Robert Stephenson & Co.

200

The world's first locomotive factory, Newcastle

1823 - 1902

and

Darlington Springfield Works

1902 - 1964

Prepared for The Robert Stephenson Trust, Charity
No. 70064

COVER IMAGE

Locomotive No 1 on the front cover was built by Robert Stephenson & Co. in 1854 for the Sydney Railway Company, New South Wales. It was the first locomotive in New South Wales and hauled the first train in 1855. After being withdrawn from service in 1877 it was preserved. Presently this locomotive has pride of place in the Powerhouse Museum, Sydney where it is displayed with 1st, 2nd and 3rd class carriages of the period. (Image copyright of The Powerhouse Museum, Sydney)

This book is dedicated to Victoria Haworth, founder trustee of The Robert Stephenson Trust, who achieved Grade II* Listed status for the historically important Works at 20 South Street, Newcastle.

Published 2022 by The Robert Stephenson Trust to celebrate the bicentenary of the creation of Robert Stephenson & Co., Newcastle upon Tyne.
ISBN 978 095 3516 209

©The Robert Stephenson Trust, 2022
Publication part funded by Newcastle City Council

Newcastle
City Council

Written and designed for The Robert Stephenson Trust by T Hugh Fenwick with support from trustees J Michael Taylor MBE and Dr Malcolm C Reed CBE

Robert Stephenson & Company's Works, Newcastle

CONTENTS

Newcastle upon Tyne Works, 1823 - 1902

Darlington Works, 1902 - 1964

The Robert Stephenson Trust

References and Acknowledgements

Robert Stephenson & Co: Locomotive Manufacturers
Bicentenary 2023
Newcastle upon Tyne Works, 1823 - 1902

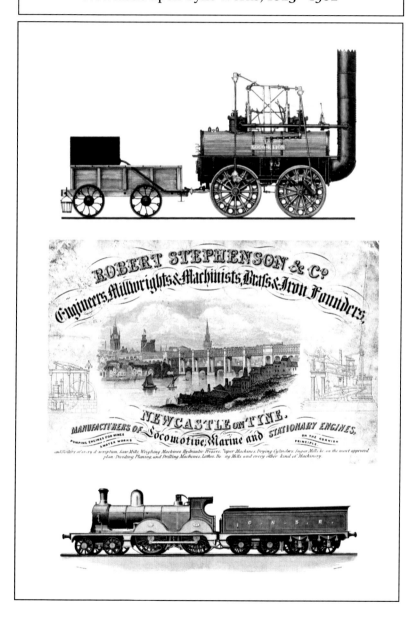

Introduction

23 June 2023 is the bicentenary of the founding of Robert Stephenson & Co. at Newcastle, the first locomotive manufacturer in the world. This pioneering company and its successors supplied locomotives to railways throughout the world over a period of more than 140 years.

The following article describes how the Robert Stephenson & Co. works at Newcastle came to be; their products; how they grew to be the pride of Newcastle; and subsequent challenges that led to their moving to a new factory built at Darlington in 1902.

The birth of Robert Stephenson & Co.

It was profit from coal in the northeast that provided the incentive and capital to develop railways. In the early 1800s colliery owners were seeking ways to improve the transport of coal and reduce the cost of moving it from pits to the river for shipping to London and elsewhere. George Stephenson was employed as enginewright for one of the largest groups of colliery owners, the Grand Allies. He had been observing "travelling engines" working in the area developed by the Middleton Railway at Leeds and by William Hedley at Wylam. In 1814 he persuaded his employers to finance him to build a locomotive at Killingworth colliery to haul coal on their wagonway to staithes on the Tyne.

George was convinced about the future of travelling engines. Over the next five year at Killingworth he continued to improve the design and construction of not only locomotives but, equally important, the track needed for these heavy machines. With the support of his employers, he obtained patents for some of these improvements. Throughout this time George's son Robert was encouraged to participate in identifying improvements, from which he gained a thorough understanding of locomotive workings. In 1819, aged sixteen, he was apprenticed to the Killingworth colliery manager Nicholas Wood.

From George's success at Killingworth he gained the reputation as the foremost railway expert in the northeast. This led to his being commissioned in 1819 to design and supervise building an eight-mile railway from Hetton colliery to the River Wear near Sunderland, the first railway in the world designed to use steam locomotives. Site work started in March 1821. He was asked also to build a number of locomotives for the railway. Robert, now eighteen, was charged with supervising their manufacture at Killingworth.

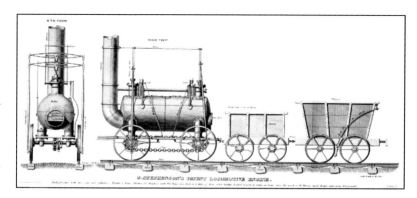

Stephenson Losh patent locomotive

Later that year George was appointed to plan the Stockton & Darlington Railway [S&DR], the world's first public railway authorised to use locomotives, and in 1822 he was tasked with building it. Edward Pease, the principal promoter of the S&DR shared George Stephenson's conviction about the future for locomotives, to the extent that in June 1823 they formed a partnership to manufacture them along with Michael Longridge, the owner of Bedlington Iron Works and young Robert.

Edward Pease lent Robert £500 towards his purchase of shares in the partnership. The company was named Robert Stephenson & Co. and Robert was made the managing partner. His first tasks were to set up the factory, equip it, hire workers and win orders for the company. The works were built at South Street in Newcastle, a developing industrial area on the north bank of the River Tyne. A cottage was converted into an office, buildings were demolished to create space for new workshops and a stationary steam engine was installed to power the heavy machinery for building the engines. The first steam engine, not a locomotive, was built for the Earl of Carlisle and despatched in December 1823.

The Stockton & Darlington Railway

At the start of 1824 orders were in progress for seven more engines, a static engine for a Mr Bragge, two engines for a steamboat and four fixed engines for the S&DR. Those for the S&DR were for hauling wagons over the proposed Brusselton and Etherley inclines at the west end of the railway. The first locomotive built by Robert Stephenson & Co. was *Locomotion*, for the S&DR. It was delivered to the railway in advance of its opening on 27 September when, driven by George Stephenson, with a train of 32 wagons and 550 passengers including the Yarm band, it attained the speed of 15 mph between Stockton and

Darlington. A local newspaper reported on 1 October 1825 that "communication by means of railways had been fully established by the experiment of that day".

Opening of the Stockton and Darlington Railway: painting by John Dobbin

Young Robert Stephenson did not see the opening of the S&DR. He had been persuaded by Edward Pease's cousin Thomas Richardson, a London financier, to take charge of the Colombian Mining Association's silver mining concessions in Colombia, South America. He had accepted a three-year contract with the Association and in June 1824 sailed from Liverpool to South America.

Robert's absence from Newcastle

Robert Stephenson & Co. [RS&Co] suffered very much from Robert's absence. Michael Longridge had to undertake management of the firm while also running his Bedlington Iron Works. While Robert was away, there was little advancement in the design of locomotives produced and there were few new orders.

Soon after Robert's departure to Columbia, George became heavily occupied with design of the Liverpool & Manchester Railway [L&MR] at the same time as he was building the S&DR. His situation was made worse by the rejection of the first Liverpool & Manchester Railway Bill by Parliament, due in part to errors in the levels carried out by George's survey team. A new survey was made by John and George Rennie who adjusted the route to appease influential objectors and the second Bill based on their survey gained Royal Assent on 1 May 1826. George was appointed Engineer to build the railway, which included the notorious crossing of Chat Moss, the massive excavation for Olive Mount cutting and a tunnel beneath the Liverpool metropolis to access the docks. The L&MR was a much more demanding project than the S&DR. By the time Robert returned to England in November 1827 George was sorely overstretched and the firm of Robert Stephenson & Co. was in a poor state.

During his journey back from Columbia Robert met Richard Trevithick, the pioneering Cornish locomotive engineer, at Cartagena. Trevithick was returning home after working in Peru, had been shipwrecked and was penniless, so Robert provided money for his passage home. Robert travelled back via New York, taking the opportunity to meet John Stevens, an American steam engine pioneer who had introduced a multitube boiler on steamboats. It can only be guessed what useful ideas about steam engine design he gathered from these encounters. What is certain is that he was now a more mature and independent person than when he left three years earlier. On his return to the Newcastle factory at the beginning of 1828 Robert's highest priorities were to revive the fortunes of the firm and improve steam engine technology to provide the fast reliable locomotives he and his father foresaw would be needed for future main line railways like the Liverpool & Manchester. He was so successful in these endeavours that within a few years the name of Robert Stephenson & Co. was famous throughout the world.

The Liverpool & Manchester Railway and the Rainhill trials

The L&MR added urgency to the development of the steam locomotive. By mid-1828 Robert had produced an improved loco, the *Lancashire Witch*. It had inclined cylinders on each side of the boiler, a double flue to increase the boiler heating area and blast pipe to draw air through the fire. Although built for the L&MR this engine was transferred instead to the Bolton & Leigh Railway for its opening on 1st August 1828. It was the start of Robert's programme to simplify design and increase heating surface to generate more steam and power.

The L&MR had been designed as a locomotive hauled railway but some of their directors did not believe locomotives could pull trains up the 1 in 96 gradients of the Whiston and Sutton inclined planes on each side of the Rainhill level. They were pressing for fixed engines to be installed. An independent report on the matter was inconclusive, so to resolve the matter they decided to hold a locomotive trial at Rainhill in October 1829 with a prize for "the most improved engine". Robert's team at Newcastle conducted a systematic appraisal of components and materials in consultation with his father, producing significant improvements to meet the requirements for the Rainhill trials. Henry Booth, the Treasurer of the L&MR, had suggested the use of a multi-tube boiler to improve heat transfer and steam generation. Robert and his team at Newcastle devised a way to manufacture it. The result was *Rocket*. As well as being the first locomotive to be fitted with a multi-tubular boiler and separate firebox, it included the successful components developed in the *Lancashire Witch*: steel leaf spring suspension and direct drive between piston and wheel crank using a crosshead, slide bars and connecting rod.

Rocket at Rainhill Bridge: painting by Alan Fearnley

The Rainhill trials drew enormous public interest. Of the many applicants for the competition there were only three real contestants: *Rocket*, *Novelty* built by Braithwaite & Ericsson, and *Sans Pareil* by Timothy Hackworth of Shildon. Both *Novelty* and *Sans Pareil* failed to complete the trials. *Rocket* was not only the clear winner: it exceeded all expectations when George Stephenson ran *Rocket* on its own across the Rainhill level and back again at what was then the astonishing speed of 35 mph. It was superior to any other locomotive at the time and was in effect the prototype of the modern locomotive. After the trials, the L&MR ordered more locomotives from RS&Co built on the principle of *Rocket*. Using the experience gained at the trials the improvement programme continued at a pace. When *Northumbrian* was delivered in August 1830 the firebox had been made an integral part of the boiler, a smokebox had been added and to reduce oscillation at speed the cylinders had been moved from inclined to almost horizontal.

Shortly after the opening of the railway in September 1830 the next development was the prototype *Planet* locomotive for the L&MR. It was more powerful and significantly different with the cylinders beneath the boiler inside the smokebox, driving the rear wheels through cranked axles. It became the first class of locomotives to be used on several of the world's earliest railways. This locomotive incorporated the principal features that would be used in steam locomotives for almost 150 years. Stephenson's ambition to change the cumbersome colliery engine to main line locomotive had been realised in less than three years, a remarkable feat. To quote Dr Michael Bailey, this achievement was one "that ranks amongst the foremost of technological advancements".

Robert Stephenson & Co. - The pride of Newcastle

The RS&Co factory was now attracting international interest with visitors from the USA, Germany and France. The works were the Pride of Newcastle. The extraordinary increase in traffic on the L&MR meant that larger and more powerful locos were needed but with low axle weights as the rails were still lightweight. Robert extended the *Planet* design over six wheels to spread the weight and took out a patent for this new generation of locomotives. The first, named *Patentee*, was completed in September 1833. This drawing shows the 1833 design for the 2-2-2 *Patentee*. Later, others were built with 0-4-2, 2-4-0 and

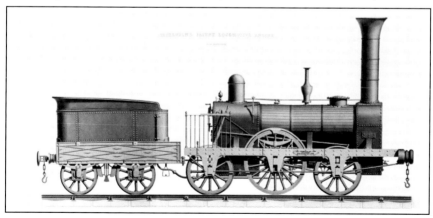

0-6-0 wheel arrangements. The Patentee design was adapted for Brunel's 7ft broad gauge Great Western Railway [GWR]. The GWR purchased two locomotives

originally built for the 5'-6" gauge New Orleans Railway but not sent because of financial complications. Instead, they were converted to Brunel's broad gauge. The first to be delivered was *North Star*, transported to Maidenhead Bridge by barge on 28 November 1837.

RS&Co *North Star* for the GWR, 1837

On 31 May 1838 it worked the inaugural train for the company's directors between Paddington and Maidenhead Bridge. This initial 22.5 mile section of the GWR was opened on 4 June 1838, operated by two of Stephenson's Patentees, *North Star* and *Morning Star*. Brunel wrote of *North Star*, "We have a splendid engine of Stephenson's. It would be a beautiful ornament in the most elegant drawing room".

The *Patentee* was generally accepted as "the best of its day". It was employed as a standard for locomotive fleets at home and abroad, including those of Belgium, Germany, France, Russia and America. Orders for *Planet* and *Patentee* locos were so numerous they had to be passed to other builders to be built under licence, as well as by the Newcastle factory. During the late 1830s the factory expanded in the Newcastle Forth Street/South Street area to meet increasing demand. The business was employing 400 workers and Robert Stephenson & Co. was the world leader in locomotive design. It was said "where there were railways, very few had no locomotives from this builder".

From mid-1833 Robert Stephenson was appointed Engineer-in-chief to design and manage construction of the London & Birmingham Railway, the biggest project ever carried out in Britain. He moved from Newcastle to London in October 1833 to oversee the work. From then until its completion in September 1838 he was very much occupied with that task, almost living on the line. Despite these pressures he remained managing partner of RS&Co, maintaining a close involvement with the Newcastle factory through correspondence and occasional visits.

The next significant development from the works was the long-boiler locomotive patented at the end of 1841. The long boiler increased the heating surface and steam generation to generate more power and speed while reducing fuel consumption. The locomotive wheelbase was kept short to fit the turntables of the time.

One of the most important innovations in locomotive design was the Stephenson Link Motion brought to perfection in 1842 by the Newcastle team. It was incorporated in the long-boiler engines and for decades after was adopted for most other locomotives throughout the world. This mechanism enabled the steam to the cylinders to be cut off and adjusted to match the power needed by the locomotive under varying conditions, to save steam and further improve fuel consumption.

Changing times

RS&Co Locomotive 'A' for the Gauge Trials, 1846

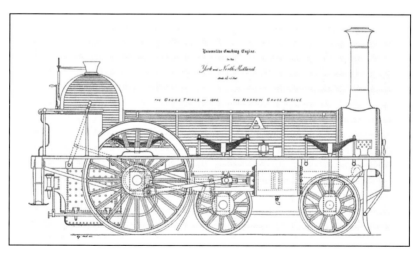

RS&Co was buoyant and profitable through the 1840's railway mania years. This period included the 1845/6 gauge commission inquiries and locomotive trials, which stimulated further improvements to Stephenson's long-boiler designs to compete with performance of the broad gauge engines. When railway mania was at its height, RS&Co had 224 engines on order.

However, by the late 1840s many other British locomotive builders had entered the market, increasing competition. Furthermore, the London & North Western, the Great Western Railway, and some other major railway companies had developed their own design capability and created workshops to manufacture locomotives, reducing demand for the British independent loco builders. From the 1850s overseas railways were being represented by consulting engineers who produced locomotive designs and specifications, which stifled the independent manufacturers' ability to win sales using their own designs. Consequently, locomotive orders were harder to find and prices were depressed. RS&Co had to diversify to survive the downturn. In addition to locomotives, they manufactured other products such as marine engines, bridge girders and large stationary engines for collieries and factories to keep the work force employed.

Towards the end of 1850 Robert sailed to Egypt in his yacht *Titania* accompanied by two associates. Following an audience with the Viceroy of Egypt, Pasha Abbas, the party explored the Suez area seeking the route for a proposed railway. Back in London in early 1851 the Pasha asked him to undertake the task of Chief Engineer to design and build this railway, the first on the continent of Africa. The project resulted in six engines being sent to Egypt from late 1852 to work on the first section of the line under construction, from Alexandria.

The company also designed and built a chain ferry for the railway to carry trains across the Nile. When completed in 1855 it was the largest item to have been fabricated at the Newcastle factory.

Increased marketing effort was put into gaining orders around the world. In 1854 RS&Co built the first locomotives for the Sydney & Goulburn Railway in Australia. One is now preserved at Sydney's Powerhouse Museum. Other orders were to come from Norway, Turkey, Ceylon, Holland, Belgium, Luxembourg and India. In 1855 the company celebrated the 1000th locomotive built since the firm's inauguration in 1823. By 1857 orders were back to 1840s levels. The largest contract comprised fifty locos built in 1857/8 for the Italian Lombardo - Venetian Railway.

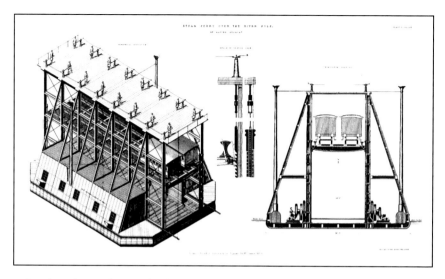

Robert's relationship with the Egyptian Pasha resulted in orders for several special locomotives for his exclusive use. The most ornate locomotive ever built by RS&Co was a 2-2-4 locomotive for the Pasha, with a luxurious saloon behind the footplate. According to a contemporary account in the Newcastle Courant, *"the exterior of the train is decorated with arabesque designs of black, white and gold, in the first style* of *art, from the designs of Mr Digby Wyatt"*. One of the Pasha's special locos and a RS&Co 0-6-0 goods engine are preserved in the Cairo railway museum.

During the 1850s and 1860s locomotive developments were mainly the use of higher boiler pressures to obtain greater engine power and the introduction of 8-wheel bogie locomotives. Between 1840 and 1850 boiler pressures raised from 50 to 75 lbs per sq.in. and from 1850 to 1860 there was a more radical increase to 130/140 lbs per sq.in. The first RS&Co 4-4-0 bogie locos were built in 1859 for the Ottoman Railway and South Australian Railways. They represented the stage of RS&Co locomotive development at the time.

South Australian Railways 4-4-0 Class D, 1859

1859 was a year of considerable change for the company. Sadly, Robert Stephenson died on 12 October, a few days before his 56th birthday, having overseen the work of the company for 36 years from its inception in 1823. His loss was felt deeply by the employees and the nation. The level of his esteem is evident by his burial in Westminster Abbey at the side of Thomas Telford, the only engineers laid to rest in the Abbey. In Newcastle on the day of his funeral the ships on the river carried their flags at half-mast; offices, shops and banks closed at noon and more than 1500 workers paid their respect by marching from the factory to St Nicholas' Church to attend a service.

Under new management

Robert's cousin George Robert Stephenson inherited Robert's shares in RS&Co and took over as the managing partner, a role he held until 1886 when the partnership changed to a private limited company. He then became chairman of the limited company until a further change in 1899, accumulating 40 years leading the business. His other partners were William Hutchinson, the Works Manager in charge of production and Joseph Pease who had inherited Edward Pease's shares.

George Robert had experience for the task. He had been employed on railway projects since 1837 with both George and Robert Stephenson. He had designed the Nile ferry. Following an incident with the ferry, when the Pasha was delayed because one of the chains broke, RS&Co was contracted to build a bridge to replace the ferry. George Robert designed a wrought iron structure that comprised two 80ft swing openings and eleven 114ft fixed spans. It was fabricated at the Newcastle factory, shipped to Egypt and opened to traffic in 1859. By 1863 the firm had fabricated 38 wrought iron bridges.

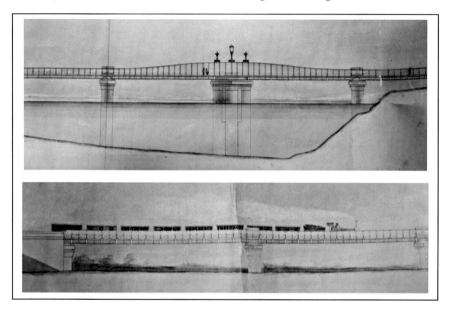

For many years the company continued to benefit from friendships and associations established earlier by Robert Stephenson. Despite major British railway companies building their own locomotives RS&Co continued to win orders from the North Eastern, Midland, London & South Western and Great Northern Railways, and from continental Europe. Over time the latter reduced significantly, particularly as continental companies set up factories that were competitors to the British firms. The situation worsened as tariffs were introduced by north European countries and America for locomotives, effectively closing those markets. To address this, like Robert before him, George Robert pursued opportunities abroad to establish new customers in Australia, New Zealand, South Africa and the Far East. From Australia he added railways in Victoria, Western Australia and Tasmania to those already served in New South Wales and South Australia.

Locomotives built during the 1860s included Great Northern Railway Sturrock designed 2-2-2s, sixty five Midland Railway 0-6-0s and 4-4-0s for the Stockton & Darlington Railway similar to those for the Ottoman Railway. Standard gauge 2-4-0 tank locos were delivered to the Cape Town Railway & Dock Company, long boiler 0-6-0s went to New South Wales and 0-4-2 locos were built for Danish Railways. One of the latter is on display at the Odense Railway Museum. Egyptian Railways continued to be a valuable customer with more locomotives being purchased between 1862 and 1868. Several engines were supplied for the 5'-3" gauge South Australian Railways, including 4-4-0 tender engines and 2-4-0 well-tank locos. Sri Lanka's first railway locomotive was *Leopold*, in 1864. It was one of five 4-4-0 locomotives built that year by Robert Stephenson & Company for the Ceylon Government Railway.

RS&Co Fitting Shop from The Illustrated London News, 1864

In the 1870s and 1880s the North Eastern Railway was one of the most important customers, with orders for fifty 0-6-0 Class 708 and eighty 0-6-0 Class 398 locomotives built between 1870 and 1876 plus other locos later. Home market customers included the London & South Western [L&SWR] and Great North of Scotland Railways [GNoSR]. The L&SWR locos were Adams designed 4-4-2 Class 415 tank engines and Class 460 4-4-0s built in the 1880s. The GNoSR engines were 2-4-0 and 4-4-0 tender engines. Overseas orders included 3'-6" gauge 2-6-0 locos for New Zealand Railways, more 5'-3" gauge locos for Australia and 5'-6" gauge 0-4-2s for the Scinde Punjab & Delhi Railway, now part of Pakistan Railways.

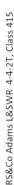

RS&Co Adams L&SWR 4-4-2T, Class 415

In 1882 RS&Co delivered the first standard gauge locomotive in China, one of two saddle tank locos built for the Kaiping Mining Bureau. It has been restored and is now on display at the Kailuan Museum in China. The same year the firm's first engine for Japan was despatched. South African Cape Government Railways ordered thirty three 4-6-0 tank-and-tender 3'-6" gauge locomotives for mainline service on all three of its systems and the Natal Government Railway procured seventeen large 4-6-0 tank engines. Several 2-6-0s were supplied to the standard gauge Central Uruguay Railway and 4-6-2 tank locos to the Bengal Nagpur Railway in India.

The diversity of engines produced by the company to satisfy customers' particular requirements was remarkable. RS&Co had to be able to deliver the proliferation of designs from customers at home and abroad. By the mid-1880s the firm had dropped from being the top independent locomotive builder in Britain to fourth, behind Neilson Reid, Dubs and Sharp Stewart, all based in Glasgow.

After the 1870s orders for locomotives had fluctuated considerably, making it difficult to maintain manning levels and determine sound investment decisions. The Newcastle works had grown piecemeal on the cramped site at South Street and there was limited opportunity to achieve economies of scale. The firm was increasingly less cost competitive against builders with spacious sites which allowed efficient factory layouts that could justify investment in production lines with the most up to date equipment. Although RS&Co product quality remained high, profitability was now the principal concern. The company was running at a loss.

The marine business

Robert Stephenson & Co. had been building marine engines and ship boilers since the 1850s when they diversified to respond to downturns in locomotive orders. They did the work at Forth Banks alongside the locomotive manufacturing. In 1864 marine engines formed an important part of the firm's output, as they were supplying marine engines for blockade-running vessels during the American Civil War. In 1869 RS&Co obtained a patent for a marine engine designed by the Works Manager, G A Crow.

The South Street site was not ideal for the marine work. It was very difficult to move large items such as ship boilers down the steep hill to the quayside. The Newcastle Chronicle reported in 1886 on the movement of a boiler weighing 65 tons from the works as being "*drawn by a team of fifty eight horses through the winding thoroughfares*. The report concluded *the ponderous pile represented an amount of concentrated labour and mechanical skill, on which the beholders might not unreasonably indulge in a little self-congratulation.*"

In 1886, to improve production methods for both the marine and locomotive businesses the company decided to lease a shipyard at Hebburn-on-Tyne, transfer the marine engine and boiler manufacturing to that yard and create space at the South Street site to improve conditions for locomotive construction. Later, in the late 1890s a lease of a further 40 acres of land at Hebburn was acquired to build a large graving dock, the largest dry dock on the north-east coast. This project suffered construction difficulties and associated contractual disputes that increased costs, significantly delayed completion and exacerbated what was already a serious loss making state of the marine business. Eventually, the entire marine business was leased in 1911 to Palmers Shipbuilding & Iron Company with an option to buy.

The end of an era

The partners changed the firm to a private limited company in 1886 to raise finance for the Hebburn shipyard and to limit the liability of the partners. However soon afterwards, because of the company's worsening financial situation, the directors of this new company had to consider whether they should close the company. In 1899 the private limited company was voluntarily wound up and a public limited company formed as Robert Stephenson & Co. Ltd. George Robert Stephenson retired, aged 80, ending the Stephenson family management of the business.

Locomotives built during these troublesome times included these elegant Manson 4-4-0 mainline locos built for the Great North of Scotland Railway, Great Northern Railway [GNR] Class J13 0-6-0 saddle tank locos (LNER Class J52) for London suburban services, forty Midland Railway Class 1121 0-6-0 tank engines and Western Australian Railways N Class 4-4-4 tank engines for suburban services around Perth. One of the GNR saddle tank locos and a Western Australian Class N have been preserved. The GNR locomotive is one of the Railway Museum's National Collection. It was built by Sharp Stewart but is to the same design as those produced by RS&Co.

The directors of the new public limited company separated the marine and locomotive businesses and decided to move locomotive building to a purpose-built factory on 54 acres of land at Darlington. Construction of the factory commenced in 1900. On completion of the Darlington factory, Robert Stephenson & Co. locomotive manufacturing activities moved from Newcastle to Darlington.

JHM McDowell photographs of the works, 1902

JHM McDowell was an electrical engineer from Manchester who was in the Newcastle area at the time of the transfer to Darlington. He had been involved with the electrification of the Newcastle corporation tramways. He contracted Robert Stephenson & Co's skilled blacksmiths to alter some of the steel poles used to support the overhead wires. Through this work he made friends with the Managing Director (G Walker) and Works Manager (WH Crow) who gave him access to take a series of photographs of the works at weekends in 1902, when the factory was in the process of running down and machines and materials were being moved to Darlington. The photographs provide a graphic record of the works at the time. Some are reproduced on the following pages., courtesy of the Stephenson Locomotive Society, to give an indication of the works immediately before closure.

The South Street entrance.

The original 1823 "Grasshopper" stationary engine that powered some of the machines in the works. It was moved to the Darlington factory for safekeeping then in 1960 was acquired by the Birmingham Museum and Art gallery.

The Frame Shop. Note the 1826 stationary engine in the background. This was smaller than the 1823 engine and to a different design. The lower photograph is a closer view of the 1826 engine.

The Low Machine Shop. The wooden crane in the upper photograph is believed to have been made by George and Robert Stephenson. It was in the oldest part of the works near the stationary engine.

The East Blacksmiths shop. The upper image shows the Orchard Street side of the blacksmiths shop. The photograph below is of the steam hammer used for forging iron wheels, rims, spokes and naves.

The High Fitting Shop over the Erecting Shop, on the west side of South Street, where components for the locomotive valve motion, etc were produced.

The Erecting Shop. The upper image is the west side of the erecting shop with a colliery engine being assembled. Below is the east side of the shop with some of the last locomotives under construction.

The following photograph is the Work's crane-tank locomotive that was used for lifting components and materials in the works area and for moving engines up the ramp to the North Eastern Railway sidings at Newcastle Central station.

The last locomotive from South Street was Robert Stephenson & Co. Works No. 3094, an 0-6-0 saddle tank for the London & India Docks Company in 1902. This ended the era of locomotive building at South Street, but a new chapter began at the new Darlington Works.

Robert Stephenson & Co. Ltd: Locomotive Manufacturers
Darlington Works, 1902 - 1964

Robert Stephenson & Co. Ltd, Darlington, 1900 to 1920

In 1899 Robert Stephenson & Co. was wound up as a private company and a new public limited company formed, Robert Stephenson and Company Limited. One of the first decisions for the new Board was to obtain more suitable accommodation and invest in modern equipment to create a viable future. They purchased fifty four acres of land at Springfield, on the north-east side of Darlington with rail connection to the nearby main line and between 1900 and 1902 built a new factory, Robert Stephenson & Co. Ltd, Darlington.

The business strategy was to produce relatively small batches of high quality locomotives to deliver their customers' requirements, using sound design and good workmanship. It was not intended to compete for high volume orders. The new works were equipped with modern manufacturing tools and laid out to deliver the strategy.

The following sections of this publication outline the activities of the new company, Robert Stephenson & Co. Ltd Darlington and attempt to show the remarkable diversity of locomotives they built between 1902 to 1964, when the last locomotive left the Darlington site.

On completion of the factory, the Robert Stephenson & Co. locomotive manufacturing activity moved from Newcastle to Darlington. In October 1902 the first locomotive was steamed within a mile of George Stephenson's Stockton & Darlington Railway, where the historic *Locomotion No 1* hauled the first train during the railway's opening on 27th September 1825.

From 1900 many British railway companies were building their own rolling stock, so most of the Darlington production was for export. Locomotives were built for railways as far afield as India, South America, Africa and Australia, with track gauges that included metre gauge, 3'-6" (1067mm) Cape gauge, 4'-8$\frac{1}{2}$" (1435mm) standard gauge and 5'-6" (1676mm) broad gauge. Locomotives ranged from small 0-4-0 saddle tanks for British dockyards to massive 2-10-0 decapods for a 5'-6" gauge Argentinian railway.

Locomotives for India and Ceylon

Railways on the Indian sub-continent were important markets for British locomotive manufacturers in the early 1900s. The Darlington works supplied locomotives to at least five Indian railways and Ceylon Government Railways. One of the first to leave Darlington in 1902 was a heavy 2-8-0 goods engine for the 5'-6" gauge Bengal Nagpur Railway [BNR]. At more than twice the weight of any locomotive from the Newcastle factory it demonstrated immediately the capability of the Springfield works.

The BNR bought several types of loco from the works. Up to the 1880s, locomotives were generally designed and built by the manufacturer. By the 1900s overseas railways were commissioning consulting engineers to specify the design requirements for their locomotives. In some cases, this comprised only a sketch showing the desired wheel arrangement, the desired heating surface and axle weights to suit the strength of bridges or permanent way. Invariably the specifications were over-optimistic, expecting the builder to squeeze a quart into a pint pot. That was the situation for the Class H 2-8-0 Bengal Nagpur Railway goods engines. Robert Stephenson & Co. Ltd produced a design that met the demanding specification and built seventeen for the BNR. These remarkable machines became the prototype for a large and successful standard class for Indian State Railways heavy freight locomotives. Soon after going into service, they were hauling coal trains of 1200 tons gross weight. Tests showed they could draw trains of 1600 tons, but the wagon couplings had to be strengthened before these could be brought into service. Locomotives of the same type were built for various Indian Railways. The photograph below shows some for the Madras and Southern Mahratta Railway being assembled in the erecting shop at Darlington.

Madras & Southern Mahratta Railway 2-8-0 at Darlington

In 1905 the company built elegant 4-6-0 locomotives for the BNR, designed by their Consulting Engineer John Wolfe Barry to reduce the running times of express mail trains between Bombay and Calcutta. The eastern half of this journey was over Bengal Nagpur metals, 701 miles (1129 km) between Nagpur and Calcutta. Most of the class bore the names of Royal Navy ships-of-the-line or battleships. Similar 4-6-0 locos were built for the 5'-6" gauge Eastern Bengal and metre gauge South Indian Railways. For the BNR RS&Co Ltd also built some sturdy 2-8-2 tank engines. As for the 2-8-0 tender engines the design details were worked up by RS&Co Ltd and subsequently the design was adopted as a standard by the Indian Standards Committee for use across the sub-continent.

ROBERT STEPHENSON & CO., Ltd.   DARLINGTON

Bengal Nagpur Railway 4-6-0

Other Stephenson built tank engines included 5'-6" gauge suburban passenger locomotives for the Ceylon Government Railway who ordered twenty Class D3 2-6-4 tank engines to handle rapidly increasing suburban passenger traffic in and around Colombo. These neat looking engines, having quick turn-around capability, were introduced for shuttle services. The power of these 75-ton machines with their 5' diameter driving wheels gave them rapid acceleration. It is said they were an impressive sight at speed, taking in their stride fully loaded 14-coach suburban trains.

ROBERT STEPHENSON & CO., Ltd.   DARLINGTON

Ceylon Government Railway Class D3

Locomotives for the rest of the world

Although the Indian sub-continent was the company's principal marketplace between 1902 and 1914, locomotives were built for railways elsewhere in the world, particularly Australia, South America, the Middle East, Asia and Africa.

Twelve narrow-gauge (3'-6") 4-4-4T Class N suburban passenger tank engines were delivered to the West Australian Railways for suburban services around Perth. These were in response to increasing traffic around Perth following the gold rush of the 1890s. The design was highly successful. Eventually forty-two were in service in both Perth and Kalgoorlie - at the height of the gold rush Kalgoorlie boasted a suburban service as frequent as that in Perth. One Class N remained in traffic on suburban passenger and shunting duties until 1960. Presently it is awaiting restoration at the Western Australian Rail Transport Museum, Perth.

Broad gauge 2-6-2T suburban and 2-8-2T goods tank engines were built for railways in Argentina. The suburban locos were for the Buenos Aires and Pacific and the Buenos Aires Southern Railways, whereas the goods engines went to the Central Argentine Railway.

A large Decapod (2-10-0 with ten coupled wheels) locomotive was built at Darlington in 1905 for the 5'-6" gauge Argentine Great Western Railway. It was the first Decapod to be built in Britain and resulted in more being ordered. The Argentine Great Western Railway joined the Ferrocarril Andino (the Andean Railway) that in turn connected with the Chilean railway system to cross the Andes and create a continuous line between the Atlantic Ocean at Buenos Aires and the Pacific at Valparaiso.

The locomotive was designed to spread its weight over the ten coupled wheels and allow it to work a line with low permissible axle loads and steep gradients. The maximum weight per driving axle was 14.5 tons, remarkably low for a loco weighing in at 135 tons with a full boiler and tender.

Compact 2-8-0 narrow-gauge engines were produced for another South American railway, the Brazilian metre-gauge Leopoldina Railway. The Leopoldina was the largest British-owned railway in Brazil. It grew to have almost 2000 miles of metre-gauge track. With its headquarters in Rio de Janeiro the railway served the three states of Rio de Janeiro, Minas Garaes, and Espirito Santo, carrying goods and passengers through mountainous country on lines with severe gradients.

Leopoldina Railway 2-8-0

Crossing now to Turkey, the Ottoman Railway Company [ORC], also known as the İzmir–Aydın Railway (Turkish: İzmir-Aydın Demiryolu), was built by a British company to transport minerals and fruit (mainly figs) from the Aydın plain to the Mediterranean Port of İzmir for export. The Ottoman Railway Company continued to operate as a regional railway until 1935, after which it was absorbed into Turkish State Railways. Standard gauge 0-8-0 locomotives for the railway were built at Darlington in 1906 and remained in use for more than 50 years. In 1911 six smart looking 0-6-0 locomotives, illustrated in this official photograph, were built for the ORC.

Ottoman Railway Company 0-6-0

Also in 1911, three 0-8-2 tank engines were built for the Ottoman Railway. The Turkish network is demanding with steep gradients and sharp curves. Consequently, high speed was not feasible so mixed traffic engines with four driving axles and small wheels were the norm for both passenger and freight trains.

South from Turkey, Sudan Government Railways on the African continent obtained 3'-6" gauge Atlantic (4-4-2) locomotives from Robert Stephenson & Co. Ltd for use on Wadi Halfa to Khartoum expresses. Wadi Halfa was founded in the

Sudan Government Railways 4-4-2

19th century as a port on the Nile for transferring goods between the railway and ferries from Aswan to provide a trade route from central Sudan north through Egypt to the Mediterranean and beyond.

Other locomotives built by RS&Co Ltd for railways on the African continent were the full class of forty five South African Railways [SAR] Class 14 Cape gauge (3'-6") 4-8-2 locomotives ordered in 1913. These were delivered in three batches between 1913 and 1915. The locos were shipped partly dismantled and re-assembled at one of the SAR workshops, steam-tested and painted before being put into traffic. They were employed on the mainline between Durban and Ladysmith in Natal. The Class 14 was the most numerous in Natal. All gave more than 60 years' service, of which more than half was on mainline duties. Later, they were transferred to mixed traffic work on secondary lines and reclassified 14R. The last was withdrawn in 1983 but three are preserved at various locations in South Africa.

South African Railways 4-8-2 Class 14

Locomotives were also supplied to railways in the Far East. These included metre gauge mixed-traffic 4-6-0 locomotives to Burma Railways for freight and passenger trains on the 385 miles between Rangoon and Mandalay. In 1913 four metre gauge Pacifics (4-6-2) were built for the Federated Malay States Railway to haul express passenger services on the Malay peninsula.

In its first fifteen years the Darlington factory produced locomotives for at least sixteen different overseas railway companies in ten countries, with eleven different wheel arrangements and four different track gauges. They included tender engines, tank engines and tank+tender engines. During the same period, they supplied customers in the home market, selling engines to more than seven

different companies in Britain with three further wheel arrangements. This wide range of products gives an indication of the capability of the Darlington works at the time. Approximately 600 locomotives were built by RS&Co Ltd between 1899 and the start of WW1 in 1914.

The home market

Home market engines included 0-4-0 tank engines for docks and collieries; London, Tilbury & Southend Railway 4-4-2 "Tilbury Tanks"; powerful 0-6-2 tanks for the Welsh Valleys Lines; NER Class P3/LNER J27 0-6-0s designed by Wilson Worsdell for the North Eastern Railway; five beautiful Wainwright 'D' 4-4-0s for the South East & Chatham Railway and six powerful Reid "Atlantics" (4-4-2 locomotives) for the North British Railway. Ten Class P3 0-6-0 locos were built for the North Eastern Railway in 1909. In the image below, RS&Co Ltd has placed

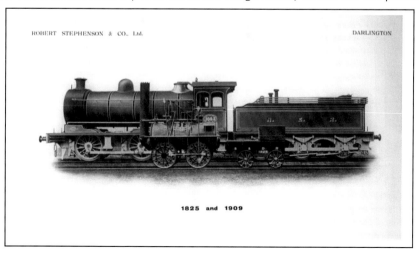

ROBERT STEPHENSON & CO., Ltd.   DARLINGTON

1825 and 1909

their first freight loco, the 1825 S&DR *Locomotion No 1*, alongside the P3 its 1909 equivalent, promoting the firm's historic descendance from the world's first locomotive factory.

World War 1

From 1910 to 1913 orders averaged about 50 locomotives per year. In 1914 and 1915, after the start of WW1, fewer locomotives were built and none was produced in 1916. Contracts for South Africa, India and elsewhere had to be suspended as the company became engaged in the war effort making gun parts, munitions and work for the Admiralty. After the war orders were sparse for almost a decade, the average output falling to approximately 20 per year, less than half the pre-war numbers. These were split about a third each between the domestic market, India and the rest of the world. Locomotive types continued to be varied as in earlier years. The following section summarises locomotives built from 1914, through the disruption of the First World War and on to 1937, the year when RS&Co Ltd purchased and took over the locomotive building part of Hawthorn Leslie and Company based at Forth Banks, Newcastle, to form Robert Stephenson and Hawthorns Ltd [RSH].

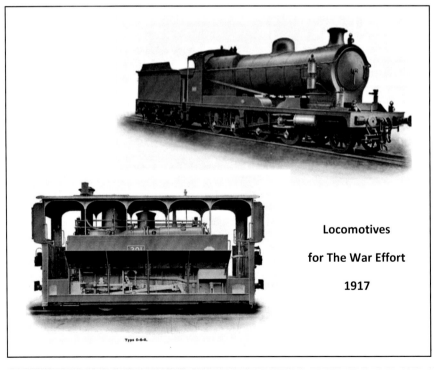

Locomotives

for The War Effort

1917

Part way through WW1, in 1917 the War Ministry urgently required locos to operate railways taken over in continental Europe. Eighty two Robinson type 2-8-0s were built by the company between 1917 and 1920 along with thirty metre-gauge 0-6-0 tram-like locomotives that serviced the trenches.

Robert Stephenson & Co. Ltd, Darlington, 1920 to 1937

The early 1920s was a period of unrest in Britain. Industrial disputes delayed production, which led to cancellation of overseas orders. The British railway company workshops were also affected by the strikes. This resulted in a large order for Robert Stephenson & Co. Ltd, thirty five 2-6-0 engines for the Great Western Railway which previously had built most of its own locomotives. Delivery commenced in 1921. These '4300' Class locos earned a reputation for being able to handle most types of traffic from local stopping goods to main line expresses, becoming the maid of all work for the Great Western.

To recover overseas sales the company increased marketing activity. Small orders started to come in from India, Africa, and Argentina Railways, supplemented with a few domestic orders. Class GS 4-6-0 locomotives were built for the 5'-6" gauge Bengal Nagpur Railway in 1920. In 1923 Sudan Railways 3'-6" gauge Pacifics were delivered for express trains between Wadi Halfa and Khartoum and between 1925 and 1929 Sudan Railways obtained thirteen 2-6-2 mixed traffic locomotives from RS&Co Ltd. A further ten 2-8-2 locomotives were also supplied around this time for the Sudan Railways Kassala extension line that had just been completed. That line went south from a junction on the Berber to Port Sudan line to Kassala, near the Eritrea border.

Domestic orders included five Class 7F 2-8-0s built in 1925 for the Somerset & Dorset Railway to supplement six built at the Midland Railway's Derby Works in 1914. These powerful locos were designed to haul both freight and passenger trains up the 1 in 50 gradients over the Mendip Hills between Radstock and Evercreech Junction. Twenty Class N7 0-6-2 tank engines were built for the LNER, the first of which was delivered in 1925. The LNER had stopped building new locomotives at Stratford due to high London wages, and pressure from the Government which was trying to ease unemployment problems in the north of England. The N7s had small wheels giving them quick acceleration, making them ideal for London suburban services. A member of the class is preserved. Great Eastern Railways No. 7999 (BR 69621) is owned by the East Anglia Railway Museum and is currently on loan to the North Norfolk Railway. A Stratford built N7 is caught in the next photograph at Liverpool Street in the 1950s.

Between1925 and 1930 the market improved with the Darlington works increasing output from about 20 locos per year to an average of 30. RS&Co Ltd started construction of six 2-8-2 Class EA locos for the metre gauge Kenya and Uganda Railway [KUR] in 1926. When built these engines were the heaviest non-articulated metre gauge locomotive in the world. After the KUR merged with

Kenya Uganda Railways Class EA "Mvita"

Tanganyika Railways in 1948 to become East African Railways the KUR EA class was renamed EAR 28 class. The photograph is of the first, No. 2801 "Mvita".

Initially these powerful machines hauled the mail trains up the spiral from Mombasa and over the 209 miles long 3290 ft (1000 m.) climb to Makindu. After the track had been strengthened with 80lb rail as far as Nairobi in 1932 they ran the full 327 miles to Nairobi. Beyond, where the track comprised 50lb rail, articulated Beyer-Garratts took over, having lighter axle weights.

In 1927 RS&Co Ltd completed a contract for sixteen South Indian Railway's mixed traffic metre gauge 4-6-0s. Transport of these locomotives from the Darlington factory to Middlesbrough Docks was arranged by the LNER, in two trains of low wagons, each consignment consisting of eight engines and eight tenders. At the docks they were craned from the wagons onto metre gauge supports on the deck of MV Belray for onward shipping to India. The engines were shipped complete in running order on October 28th, 1927.

From 1927 twelve handsome Ceylon Government Railways Class B1 broad gauge (5' 6") 4-6-0s were built by RS&Co Ltd. They represented the finest and most versatile steam locomotive type on the island, hauling fast expresses and the heaviest goods trains during the steam era. Some were converted to oil-firing in the latter days of steam. In 1928 RS&Co Ltd produced also for Ceylon Government Railways several 0-6-2 tank engines (Class E1) and 2-6-4 tank engines (Class D1). Ten broad gauge compound 2-8-2s were built for the Central Argentine Railway, one of the Big Four British broad gauge railway networks in Argentina.

1929 and 1930 were reasonably good years for RS&Co Ltd, with the company delivering locomotives to Turkey, India, Malaysia and South America plus a very special locomotive for the USA. Six magnificent 2-8-2s were built for the standard gauge Ottoman Railway between 1929 and 1932. These engines were taken over by Turkish Railways in 1935 and operated into the 1990s. The photograph is of one in the Izmir area.

Ottoman Railway 2-8-2 at Izmir

An unusual and special contract came from the USA in 1929, the centenary year of the success of Stephenson's *Rocket* at the Rainhill trials. Henry Ford commissioned Robert Stephenson & Co. Ltd to produce an "as exact as possible" replica of *Rocket*. Henry Ford wanted to mark the centenary by creating four replicas to be built by RS&Co Ltd that could go into museums around the world to teach the public not only what it looked like but how it worked. Hence,

Rocket replica built for Henry Ford in 1929

two of the four locos created on his initiative were sectioned replicas. The other two were to be working replicas. The first, delivered in 1929, is in the Henry Ford Museum at Dearborn, Michigan. The other working replica is on display at the Chicago Museum of Science & Industry.

One sectioned replica was presented to the New York Museum of Peaceful Arts but is now privately owned somewhere in the USA. The second sectioned replica was presented to the London Science Museum and is now displayed in the Railway Museum at York.

The world recession in the 1930s brought about the demise of Palmer's shipyard on the Tyne in 1934, which in turn precipitated the Jarrow March of October 1936. Most industries throughout Britain and the developed world suffered the effects of the depression. RS&Co Ltd was no exception. Production from 1931 to 1935 reached an all-time low of about 15 locomotives per annum. They were difficult years for the company. From 1931 to 1934 there were no significant orders.

It must have been a welcome relief when Robert Stephenson and Co. Ltd won an order to supply South African Railways with impressive 3'-6" gauge Class 15E 4-8-2 Mountain type mixed traffic locomotives. This was the start of the era of big locomotives in South Africa. As the railways were largely single line with passing places and trains running at infrequent intervals, very large engines were needed to haul long heavy trains. In 1935, Robert Stephenson and Co. Ltd delivered twenty of these locomotives.

South African Railways Class 15E

Orders in 1936 included seven metre-gauge 2-6-4 tank engines for the South Indian Railway and five Pacifics for Madras & Southern Mahratta metre gauge lines. These were some of the last locomotives to be built by the firm Robert Stephenson & Co. Ltd.

Madras & Southern Mahratta Pacific

On 1 January 1937, the company bought the locomotive department of Hawthorn Leslie & Co. Ltd at Forth Banks, Newcastle. The two firms were amalgamated under the name of Robert Stephenson & Hawthorns Ltd. Both needed to consolidate and cut their overhead costs to survive in the much reduced market. At the time of the merger RS&Co had built 4,155 engines and Hawthorn Leslie & Co. 2,783 making a joint total of 6,938. Hence, the Works Numbers of locomotives produced by Robert Stephenson and Hawthorns [RSH] started with 6,939.

Robert Stephenson & Hawthorns Ltd – 1937 to 1944

The new company's policy was to concentrate building of main line locomotives at Darlington and industrial locomotives at the Hawthorn's Forth Banks factory, although some industrial locos were built at Darlington depending on workload at the two sites. Eleven B17 *Sandringham* Class 4-6-0s had been ordered by the LNER in February 1936 from RS&Co Ltd (LNER numbers 2862 to 2872; BR numbers 61662 to 61672). These were delivered between January and July 1937, immediately after the firm became Robert Stephenson & Hawthorns [RSH]. They were intended for use in the North Eastern area of the LNER but initially were allocated to the Great Central lines. Later they were reallocated to the Great Eastern lines. Most were named after football teams in the east midlands or the north of England.

The loco *Tottenham Hotspur* changed names twice. When built in May 1937 it was *Manchester City* but was immediately changed to *Tottenham Hotspur* before being photographed at the Darlington works as shown below. Four months later in September 1937, it was changed again to *City of London*, the name it carried until withdrawn in April 1960.

RSH entered the diesel market in November 1937 with a "direct reversing" locomotive fitted with a Crossley two-stroke engine. There was no reversing gearbox and the diesel engine itself was reversible, as in marine practice. When starting, in either direction, power was supplied by compressed air until the engine fired. One of these locomotives, *Beryl* (RSH Works number 7697, built in 1953), is preserved at the Tanfield Railway.

In 1938 RSH bought the goodwill of Leeds companies Kitson & Co. Ltd and Manning Wardle. This included the ingenious design for Kitson-Meyer 2-8-8-2 articulated tank locomotives with two "engines" mounted under the boiler. RSH built one for Colombian National Railways in South America to work the steeply graded and sinuous 3-ft gauge Giradot Lines. A photograph of the loco was included in RSH promotional literature. One can only speculate what Robert Stephenson would have thought of this, having worked nearly three years in Columbia from 1824 to 1827 during his formative years, when railways were only in their infancy at home.

Kitson-Meyer 2-8-8-2 articulated loco for Colombian National Railways

Around 1938 RSH built some fast and powerful broad gauge Bengal Nagpur Railway Class GSM 4-6-0s for use on express passenger trains between Calcutta and Nagpur. It is likely they were to replace the 4-6-0s built by RS&Co Ltd in 1905.

Bengal Nagpur Railway Class GSM 4-6-0

From 1938 and during World War 2 the works were occupied building 0-4-0 and 0-6-0 saddle tanks for collieries, steelworks and other industries. An extraordinary order during the hostilities was four oil-fired standard gauge streamlined PC class 4-6-2s for Iraqi State Railways in 1941, one of which was lost at sea en-route to Iraq. They were built for express passenger trains between Baghdad and Tel-Kotchek 330 miles to the north, on the Syrian border.

Very few other orders were obtained from abroad during World War 2 but between 1943 and 1945, as a sub-contractor to the Hunslet Engine Company, Robert Stephenson & Hawthorns built ninety Austerity 0-6-0 saddle tank locomotives for the War Department. After the war seventy five were bought by the LNER in 1945/46 and transferred to British Railways at nationalisation in 1947 to become their Class J94. Most of the remainder went to the National Coal Board.

Austerity 0-6-0ST in British Railways livery

In 1944 an overhead electric 550V DC Bo-Bo shunter was built at the RSH Newcastle works for Kearsley Power Station in Lancashire. It was the continuation of an earlier Hawthorn Leslie design, one of four delivered between 1928 and 1945. This locomotive was used at Kearsley until 1982 when the CEGB rebuilt it as a battery loco and moved it to Heysham Nuclear Power Station. British Energy

withdrew it in 2009. It is now preserved at the Electric Railway Museum, Coventry.

Vulcan Foundry Ltd acquired Robert Stephenson & Co. Ltd, 1944

The Vulcan Foundry merged with RSH in 1944 by acquiring a substantial shareholding in the company. However, the Darlington and Newcastle factories continued to do business under the name of Robert Stephenson & Hawthorns Ltd. The merger brought together Robert Stephenson & Co. and the Vulcan foundry established in 1830 by Robert Stephenson and Charles Tayleur to meet the high demand for locomotive building following the opening of the Liverpool & Manchester Railway. After the 1944 merger the bulk of the output from RSH continued to be industrial customers, supplemented with larger locos for export and, between 1949 and 1953, batches of steam locos for British Railways.

An order for Darlington in 1947 was the first fifty post-war South African Railways 3'-6" gauge Class 19D 4-8-2 locomotives, numbered in the range from 2721 to 2770. The RSH team that built them pose for a group photograph on No. 2726.

The Class 19D was the most numerous South African branch line locomotive and, at 235 built for the SAR, was only twenty fewer than the Class 15F mainline locomotive, the most numerous South African steam class. The Class 19D was very versatile and saw main and branch line service across South Africa with the exception of the Western Cape, where the Class 19C was used. On occasion, South African Class 19Ds worked through from Mafeking in South Africa via Botswana to Bulawayo in Zimbabwe.

South African Railways Class 19D 4-8-2

South African Railways [SAR] placed orders for the design and construction of 3 kV DC Class 3E Co-Co electric locomotives with Metropolitan-Vickers in 1944. Although the locomotive was designed by Metropolitan-Vickers, who also supplied the electrical equipment, construction was subcontracted to Robert Stephenson & Hawthorns. Twenty-eight locomotives were delivered in 1947 and 1948. The Class 3E was SAR's first six-axle electric locomotive. It was geared for a maximum speed of 105 kmph (65 mph). The locos were designed for both goods and passenger working on the Western Transvaal System, where higher speeds were possible on track with flatter curves than the Natal mainline.

South African Railways Class 3E Co-Co electric

In 1948, RSH built some impressive 5'-6" gauge 4-8-0 steam locos for the Central Argentine Railway [Ferrocarril Central Argentino]. Ten metre gauge Class YB Pacifics were built in 1948-9 for the Indian Jamnagar and Dwarka State Railways. Other orders were received and delivered to Burma, Tasmania, Jordan, Tanganyika, New Zealand and Australia. Good times had returned for the firm with orders of around 70 locos per year between 1945 and 1950. RSH built more than twenty metre gauge Class ST 2-6-4T engines for Burma Railways between 1947 and 1949. Those built at RSH's Newcastle works were taken by road on a low-loader to Liverpool for onward shipping to Rangoon. The photographs below show the transporter crossing the Tyne Bridge and negotiating streets through the city of York.

The home market provided two sizeable orders from British Railways [BR] in 1949. The first was for thirty five Class L1 2-6-4 tank engines built in 1949 and 1950 for the Eastern Region. The second was for eighty BR Western Region 0-6-0 Class 9400 pannier tanks, built between February 1950 and January 1953. A further twenty of these locomotives were built by RHS as subcontractors to Hudswell Clarke. There are no surviving Class L1 locos but two Class 9400 are preserved. Number 9400, one of the last steam engines to be built at Swindon Works, is at the Swindon Steam Railway Museum and 9466, built by RSH, is still operational at the Ecclesbourne Valley Railway in Derbyshire.

British Railways Class L1 2-6-4T

In the post-war period, in addition to the overseas and British Railways orders RSH produced many industrial engines for the home market, comprising steam, diesel and electric shunters. A further 550V DC electric Bo-Bo was built for

Central Electricity Authority 0-6-0T No. 12

Kearsley Power station. Powerful 0-6-0 saddle tanks, a development of the "Austerity", were supplied to the NCB and Dorman Long's Lackenby works. The two largest were saddle tank locomotives for Richard Thomas & Baldwin's Ltd Ebbw Vale Steelworks. In the 1950s, six-coupled side tanks engines were made for the British Electricity Authority, based on a 1936 design by Hawthorn Leslie for Birmingham Power Station. A 300HP diesel mechanical 0-6-0 shunter was built in 1951 for the British Electricity Authority's Carrington Power Station.

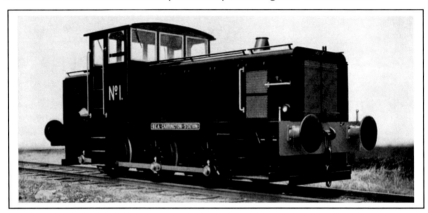

Seven1500V DC overhead electric locos were built by RSH during 1951/2 in collaboration with English Electric Co. Ltd for New Zealand Railways [NZR]. These 3'-6" gauge Class EW locomotives were for use on the Wellington suburban network. They were the most powerful locomotives in New Zealand for twenty years. In addition to working passenger trains in the Wellington area, they acted as banking engines for trains between Paekakariki and Pukerua Bay. The class was

New Zealand Railways 1500V-DC Class EW

well-liked by drivers as NZR had worked closely with them in establishing the design of the EW class, which led to the cabs being laid out to make them easy to operate. They were reliable locomotives capable of generating twice their specified power output as was evidenced by a NZR engineer during tests in the 1960s when EW 1806 produced a power output of 3,600 hp (2,700 kW). One of the class is preserved and restored at Wellington.

International steam locos built in the first half of the 1950s included six metre-gauge Pacifics for the Indian Bikaner State Railway, to the Indian Railways Standard Class YB/2 design, built by RSH in 1951. Another ten narrow gauge (3'-6") Pacifics were delivered to Tasmanian Government Railways in March 1952. Similar to the Indian Railways YB class, the Tasmanian Railways M-Class were allocated to operate on Tasmania's North-Eastern and Western lines and at Hobart. However, dieselisation was being introduced on some of these lines. Consequently in 1957 four were fitted with smaller driving wheels recovered from withdrawn Australian Garratts, enabling them to operate heavier trains over the steeply graded North-Eastern line. As they became due for overhaul from 1960, they were withdrawn with the last removed from traffic in 1975. One is preserved at the Tanfield Railway.

This photograph shows the ten Tasmanian locos awaiting shipment to Hobart by MV Christen Smith (Bel-Line vessel) at Middlesbrough in early 1952.

In 1952 six metre-gauge Tanganyika Railways ML class 2-8-2 freight locos were shipped to East Africa. The engines had been ordered from Robert Stephenson in 1947 but were delivered in 1952 after Tanganyika Railways had become part of

East African Railways [EAR], when they were redesignated EAR Class 26. Three other 2-8-2 locos were built for the Hedjaz Railway (Jordan) in 1952. These were oil-fired and operated on part of the old Hedjaz Railway linking Damascus and Medina.

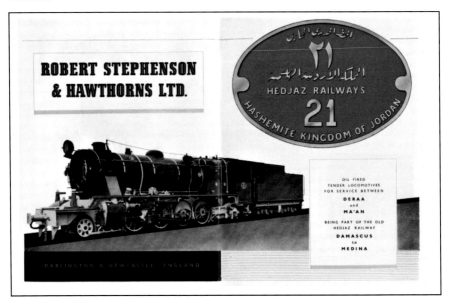

Broad gauge (5'-6") Indian Railways Class WM 2-6-4 tank engines were built in 1953/4 for the Indian Government Railways. The Class was introduced in 1942 and eventually totalled 70 new engines, thirty of which were from RSH.

Indian Railways Class WM 2-6-4T

Western Australia Government Railways [WAGR] ordered twenty four V Class 2-8-2 locomotives from Beyer, Peacock & Co, Manchester in 1951. Due to capacity issues Beyer, Peacock subcontracted construction of these impressive machines to Robert Stephenson & Hawthorns Darlington works in 1955. The V class was the last steam class of to enter service with WAGR. They were built to haul heavy coal traffic between the Collie coal fields and Perth as part of a post-war regeneration plan for WAGR. The locomotives entered service between April 1955 and November 1956.

West Australia Government Railways V Class 2-8-2

The final years, 1955 to 1964

In March 1955, the Vulcan Foundry Ltd including RSH was purchased by English Electric Co. Ltd. English Electric then had works at Newton-le-Willows, Darlington, Newcastle, Bradford and Preston as main centres of their railway traction division. After 1955 there were few significant overseas orders for RSH. Between 1955 and 1958 production comprised mainly industrial tank engines of one form or another.

The last conventional steam locomotive made by RSH was an 0-6-0 saddle tank in October 1958 for Stewarts & Lloyd. At Darlington production was moving to small diesel shunters. Fifteen 107 hp 'Husky' diesel mechanical engines were built, seven of which were exported. The bottom right image below is a 'Husky' supplied to British Industrial Sand, Redhill, in 1958. Another was bought by Ashmore, Benson & Pease, Stockton.

The very last RSH steam locomotive was a six-coupled fireless locomotive ordered by the NCB for their Glasshoughton Coking Plant, delivered in January 1959. As explained in the advertisement below, the loco reservoir was charged with steam from a stationary boiler, which enabled it to be used at locations where there was risk of explosion or where cleanliness of operation was essential.

CHARGE
with steam—*and drive away!*

The STEPHENSON-HAWTHORN fireless steam locomotive is simplicity itself in operation—just charge the reservoir with steam and to work it goes! Of robust construction throughout yet with only three simple controls, it can be operated without special training.

It is eminently suitable for intermittent shunting duties and where it is essential to eliminate risk of fire or explosion, or in smoke abatement areas.

The initial cost is low and due to its simple design, maintenance is reduced and cost of repairs and overhauls is minimised.

Wherever a supply of saturated or superheated steam is available, the STEPHENSON-HAWTHORN fireless locomotive can be quickly put to work. *Send for technical information to:*

ROBERT STEPHENSON & HAWTHORNS LTD

DARLINGTON AND NEWCASTLE UPON TYNE

Partners in Progress in The ENGLISH ELECTRIC Group

The first Robert Stephenson & Hawthorn fireless locomotive was ordered in 1941 by the Northmet Power Station Co. Ltd and delivered on 9th October 1942 to Neasden Generating Station, London. The yellow loco in the group of illustrations is one of two fireless locos built in the 1950s for the large North Thames Gas Board's Beckton gasworks in east London. They were in use up to 1970 when North Sea gas brought an end to these large establishments.

Closure of RSH Newcastle Works, 1960

The Newcastle Forth Banks works closed in 1960 and all diesel and electric locomotive building was concentrated at Darlington. Forth Banks works established in 1823 by Robert Stephenson & Co. adjoined the works of R&W Hawthorn Ltd so an important link with the past was severed at what was virtually the birthplace of the locomotive.

The Darlington factory had converted exclusively to diesel and electric loco production, principally for the British Railways modernisation programme, building Class 04 shunters and the larger Class 20, Class 40 and Class 37 diesel locomotives. These orders kept the factory working to capacity from 1958 to 1962.

The 04s were 0-6-0 diesel-mechanical shunting locomotives. RSH started building them in 1955/6, soon after joining English Electric Co. Ltd. Contractually they were supplied to British Railways by the Drewry Car Co., which at the time and

British Railways Class 04 diesel mechanical shunter

for most of its existence had no manufacturing capability. Drewry sub-contracted manufacture of the locos to the Vulcan Foundry and Robert Stephenson & Hawthorns. One hundred and forty two were built for BR and two for the Central Electricity Generating Board.

The Class 20, also known as the English Electric Type 1, comprised 1000hp Bo-Bo diesel-electric freight locomotives. Two hundred and twenty eight were built by the English Electric Group between 1957 and 1968 in two phases: Phase 1 from 1957 to 1962 and phase 2 from 1965 to 1968. The large number of Class 20s and the phasing were partly a result of the failure of other manufacturers to provide reliable locomotives in the same power range in the early years of British Rail's dieselisation. The Class 20s often operated in pairs as visibility from the driving cab was very limited when travelling with the cab at the rear. A pair is seen here leading a train of empty limestone hoppers from British Steel, Redcar to Redmire for re-loading. The first of the Class, D8000, is preserved in the National Collection at the National Railway Museum.

British Railways Class 20 diesel electric freight loco

Two hundred 2000hp Class 40 1-Co-Co-1 locos were built by English Electric between 1958 and 1962. When introduced they were numbered D200-D399 and for a time were the pride of British Rail's early diesel fleet. The Class 40 derived from the prototype diesel locomotives LMS numbers 10000 and 10001 ordered by the London, Midland and Scottish Railway in 1947 and from the British Railways Southern Region No. 10203, which was powered by English Electric engines developing 2,000 bhp. The bogie design and power pack of 10203 were used almost unchanged on the first ten production Class 40s.

In this photograph Class 40 No. D237 is being finished at the Darlington works alongside a metre gauge East African Railways & Harbour Commission (EAR&H] Class 90. This was EAR&H's first order for mainline diesel locomotives. A 13.5 ton maximum axle loading was specified to enable the locomotives to work northwest of Nairobi to Nakuru and Kampala, as well as between Mombasa and Nairobi, where there was a higher permissible axle weight. The low axle load required the weight of the loco to be spread over eight axles, resulting in them having a 1-Co-Co-1 wheel arrangement, the same as for the Class 40.

Despite the initial success of the Class 40s, by the time the last were entering service they were already being replaced on East Coast principal trains by the more powerful Class 55 *Deltics* introduced in 1961/2. RSH built twenty Class 40s in 1960/61, D305 to D324, the last being completed in July 1961. Two of those built by RSH are preserved (D306 and D318). One is at the East Lancashire Railway and the other at Tyesely Loco Works.

English Electric Co. Ltd, Stephenson Works, Darlington, 1962

As from 1 January 1962 the name of the Darlington works was changed to ENGLISH ELECTRIC CO. LTD, Stephenson Works, Harrowgate Hill, Darlington, retention of the Stephenson name acknowledging the origins of the company and of locomotive building by George and Robert Stephenson.

By 1962 nearly all production at Darlington was English Electric Type 3 diesel-electric (British Rail Class 37) general purpose locomotives. English Electric Co. Ltd built more than three hundred of these 1750hp Co-Co locomotives at Darlington and the Vulcan Foundry between 1960 and 1965. Sixty seven were built at Darlington, for three orders. The first, in February 1960 was for ten locomotives, followed in April 1961 for seventeen more, with the final order of forty in December 1961. The Class 37 was one of British Railways' most successful and versatile diesel locos. They could be seen on many parts of the British rail network on freight and passenger trains. Some are still in use with Network Rail, Colas Rail and Direct Rail Services.

Sadly, in 1964 the last locomotive left the Darlington factory. British Railways Class 37 D6898 ended 141 years of locomotive building by Robert Stephenson & Co. and its descendants. This photograph is from that day.

Robert Stephenson & Hawthorns Ltd continued to be a registered company until renamed RSH Realisations Ltd in July 2005 and finally dissolved on 7 July 2008. After closure the Darlington factory was demolished and now the site is a housing estate. The houses that were built near the factory in the early 1900s for the company's employees remain. Thankfully, the War Memorial to the men from the works who fell in the Great War 1914-1918 was rescued. It is now at Darlington's Head of Steam Museum.

The last locomotive from the works is now on display close by The Head of Steam Museum. It was returned to Darlington in 2021, when it was gifted to the town by the final owner, Network Rail.

Postscript

After RS&Co Newcastle locomotive building moved to Darlington in 1902 the original Newcastle factory buildings, started in 1823 at South Street, were taken over by the motor trade until 1970.

The Robert Stephenson Trust

In 1988 the Robert Stephenson Trust was formed to save what remained of the Newcastle Robert Stephenson & Co. locomotive works. By 2003 that aim had been realised. The original office block and a workshop at 20 South Street were restored and repaired by the Trust. Listed Building status was obtained in 2005 to secure the buildings into the future, a monument to the ingenuity and dedication of those who developed and built locomotives over a period of 141 years, at both Newcastle and Darlington.

Robert Stephenson was one of the greatest engineers of all time. He is one of only two engineers buried in Westminster Abbey. Robert, with his father George and other associates, designed and built railways and manufactured locomotives that changed the world. The Trust's Vision is to make todays and future generations aware of the achievements of Robert Stephenson, his father George, his other associates, and their contribution to modern society.

The Purpose of the Trust

The purpose of the Robert Stephenson Trust is:

- to promote, maintain, improve and advance public education and knowledge of the development of railways, and in particular of the role of Robert Stephenson, his Companies, Partnerships and other interests, and the City of Newcastle upon Tyne in that development.

- to preserve for the benefit of the residents of the City of Newcastle upon Tyne in the County of Tyne and Wear and the nation at large, whatever of the English historical, architectural and constructional heritage as may exist in and around the City aforesaid, particularly that concerned with the development of railways in the form of buildings (including any building as defined in Section 290(1) of the Town and Country Planning Act 1971)of particular beauty or historical or constructional interest.

Want to be involved?

The approach of the bicentenaries of a series of key railway events is a spur to action. The formation of Robert Stephenson & Co. took place in 1823 and provided the locomotives for the first public railway authorised by Parliament to use such motive power when the Stockton & Darlington Railway opened in 1825. The design of *Rocket* by Robert Stephenson, which won the Rainhill speed and performance trials in 1829, established the basic principles for future steam locomotive designs. In like manner the successful completion of the Liverpool &

Manchester Railway, the first inter-city railway, transformed travel throughout the world. This led to Robert's appointment in 1834 as the Engineer for the largest project ever attempted in the UK at the time, the London & Birmingham Railway, followed by many others. These bicentenaries present crucial opportunities for publicity and information dissemination.

Members of The Robert Stephenson Trust are people who support the Trust. Some look after our collections and displays, some staff our stands at public events, some are active in researching the associated history, but such activities are not requirements for membership. Members receive our bi-annual Newsletter *'Rocket'* and enjoy some discounts on our other publications.

If you wish to be involved either as a regular subscriber or as an active helper/volunteer or similar, you are invited to join. Subscriptions

support the Trust's activities and help to improve its collection of items for display and preservation. Or you may care to widen your involvement by offering your time to assist with various events.

If you would like to know more, please Email the Trust for further details,

rstrust@robertstephensontrust.com

References

Addyman, John, and Haworth, Victoria (2005), *Robert Stephenson: Railway Engineer.*

Bailey, Michael R, (ed) (2008), *Robert Stephenson – The Eminent Engineer.*

Bailey, Michael R (2021), Built in Britain - *The Independent Locomotive Manufacturing Industry in the Nineteenth Century.*

Dean, Chris, *Robert Stephenson & Company: A Financial Basket Case?*

Howarth, Victoria (2004), *Robert Stephenson: Engineer and Scientist – The Making of a Prodigy 1803-1859.*

Longridge, Bob (2016), *Rocket Man with Cousin Jacks – Robert Stephenson in Colombia 1824-1827.*

Lowe, James W (1975), *British Steam Locomotive Builders.*

Warren, JGH (1923), *A Century of Locomotive Building by Robert Stephenson & Co. 1823-1923.*

Acknowledgements

Where known, copyright of the images is acknowledged as follows:

Cover image, The Powerhouse Museum, Sydney; page 1(bottom), Illustrated London News; page 3 (top), Science and Society Picture Library; page 3 (bottom), LNER Encyclopaedia; page 8, Alan Fearnley; page 10, Science and Society Picture Library; page 13 (top), ICE Publishing; page 16, Illustrated London News; page 19, LNER Encyclopaedia; pages 20 to 25 inclusive, JHM McDowell Trust.

Most of the images for the period after 1902 are taken from promotional literature produced by Robert Stephenson & Co. Ltd and successor companies. The image on page 27 (bottom) is from The Northern Echo; page 28, Historic England; page 38 (top), Steve Armitage; page 45 (bottom), Hugh Llewelyn; page 54 (top, left), Tanfield Railway; page 54 (top, right, lower), Gordon Edgar; page 54 (bottom, right, upper), Gordon Edgar; page 54 (bottom, right, lower), RC Riley; page 55, Charlie Jackson; page 56, Rail Photoprints.